TRAIL MAKER

TRAIL MAKER

The Story of David Livingstone

by
ROBERT O. LATHAM

LUTTERWORTH PRESS
GUILDFORD, SURREY

First paperback edition 1980

Second impression 1983

To
JOHN AND DAVID

ISBN 0 7188 2489 X

PRINTED PHOTOLITHO IN GREAT BRITAIN
BY EBENEZER BAYLIS AND SON, LTD.
THE TRINITY PRESS, WORCESTER, AND LONDON

CONTENTS

		Page
1	THE BOY OF BLANTYRE	7
2	DAVID AND THE LION	12
3	ON TO THE NORTH	18
4	THE FIRST GREAT TRAIL	28
5	FROM WEST TO EAST	45
6	SLAVES ON THE ZAMBEZI	59
7	ALONE IN AFRICA	80

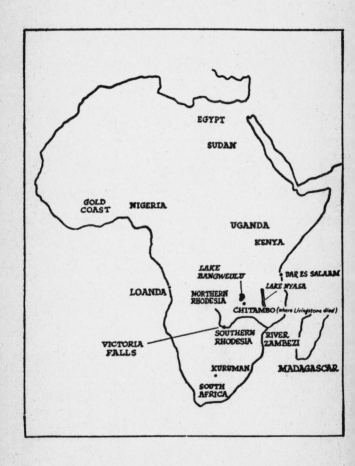

EGYPT

SUDAN

GOLD
COAST   NIGERIA

UGANDA

KENYA

*LAKE
BANGWEULU*   • DAR ES SALAAM

LAKE NYASA

LOANDA   NORTHERN
RHODESIA

CHITAMBO (*where Livingstone died*)

VICTORIA
FALLS   SOUTHERN
RHODESIA   RIVER
ZAMBEZI

• KURUMAN   MADAGASCAR

• SOUTH
AFRICA

1

THE BOY OF BLANTYRE

"PUT out that light, and go away to bed, David."

"Yes, Mother, in a minute. I've another page to learn."

"No, laddie, it's the middle of the night, and you've to be in the mill by six."

Mrs. Livingstone jumped out of bed and snatched the book away from him. She blew out the paraffin lamp, and the only light left in the little kitchen was the dull glow of the dying embers of the fire. He heard his mother get back into bed, and then quickly undressing he lay down by his brothers on the bed on the floor, and was soon asleep.

At half-past five Mrs. Livingstone was waking her sleeping family, and stirring the porridge for breakfast. As David left the house for the mill across the road, he picked up his book again and took it with him. His job at the mill was to watch the machines as they spun the cotton thread, and when the thread broke, he had to piece it together again. He worked with his book propped up against the machine, and in this way he learnt his Latin verbs and nouns by heart. The girls in the mill teased him and tossed bobbins at his book, but for most of the long working day, from six in the morning till eight at night, he read as he worked.

By the time he was sixteen he had read Virgil and Horace and knew much of them off by heart. He enjoyed reading books on travel and science, too, and he could not get hold of enough of them.

When he was about twenty he read a missionary magazine asking for doctors to go to China. David felt that God was calling him to be a doctor and go out perhaps to China.

So he studied in Glasgow University during the winter months, and worked in the Blantyre mills in the summer, to earn enough money to pay his way.

At the end of 1839, he applied to be a missionary of the London Missionary Society and he was called down to London to meet the directors of the Society. They sent him for three months' training to the Rev. Richard Cecil in Chipping Ongar, Essex.

Mr. Cecil taught his students to learn their sermons off by heart, so that they could preach without notes. One Sunday evening David set out to preach at the little village church of Stamford Withers. All went well until the sermon came. He announced the text, and read it out, then his mind went blank. He couldn't remember a word! There he stood in the pulpit awkward, embarrassed and silent. Then suddenly he blurted out, "Friends, I have forgotten all I had to say." He came down from the pulpit, and hurried out of the chapel, feeling very ashamed.

The report on David Livingstone sent in by Mr. Cecil was not a very good one, but after a further three months he was accepted by the Missionary Society and told to complete a medical course in London.

London was an exciting place in those days. Slavery had just been abolished in the British colonies, but in 1840 meetings were held in London to protest against the slave trade in Africa. One meeting was addressed by Robert Moffat, just home from South Africa. "I have seen the smoke of a thousand villages," he said, "where the Gospel has not yet been proclaimed." David was stirred as he listened and went up to Dr. Moffat after the meeting. "Dr. Moffat," he said, "do you think I would do for Africa?" "Yes, if you are ready to push on to the north." This was exactly what David wanted.

He hurried home to Blantyre to say goodbye. The family gathered round the fire in the little room in Shuttle Row one cold November night, and there David told them all that he had heard about Africa, and all that he hoped to do. Before they went to bed his father handed David the family Bible, and asked him to lead the family prayers. David turned to Psalm 121, and read:

*The Lord is thy keeper: the Lord is thy
    shade upon thy right hand.*
*The sun shall not smite thee by day nor
    the moon by night.*
*The Lord shall preserve thy going out and
    thy coming in from this time forth and
    even for evermore.*

Early next morning he set off for London
and in the last days of November 1840 he sailed
for Africa.

2

DAVID AND THE LION

WHEN he arrived at Cape Town David bought in stores and equipment, guns and ammunition, and then sailed round the coast to Algoa Bay. From there he set off in a Cape wagon with a span of oxen on the five hundred mile trek to Kuruman, his new home. For six glorious weeks David travelled and camped across the African veldt and reached Kuruman on July 31, 1841. The journey from London had taken just over seven months.

His first job was to learn the language, and with an older missionary, Roger Edwards, to make short trips to the north in search of a site where they could open up new work. They travelled over seven hundred miles through unexplored country in the first year. David made a special visit to one tribe which was known to be unfriendly, and which a few years earlier had poisoned a white trader and two of his men. He was the first white man to visit them since the murder and when he walked boldly into their village all but the chief and his two attendants fled. He sat down beside them and talked quietly, but he saw fear and terror on their faces. Timidly they offered him food to eat, and although they had poisoned the last white man, he ate it and then lay down to sleep. The chief and his people saw that he trusted them and they were quick to be friendly.

For two years David lived at Kuruman, but was always eager to push on to the north. On one trip he took some new "African companions", as he called them. He heard them whispering about him.

"He is thin," they said. "He is not strong. He only appears stout because he puts himself into those bags (trousers). He will soon knock up."

David wrote, "This made my highland blood rise, and although I was tired I kept them all walking at top speed day after day, until I heard them saying, 'although he is thin, he is a strong walker.' "

At last in June 1843 he received a letter from London giving him permission to build a new station in the northern villages.

"I am willing to go anywhere provided it be forward," he said. He chose a beautiful place called Mabotsa about two hundred miles north of Kuruman where the country was hilly and wooded, with plenty of people in the villages and plenty of wild animals too. But the people were not friendly. They refused to help him, so he and the men he had brought with him from Kuruman had to build the mission house alone.

Almost every day the district was raided by lions. They killed many cattle at night, and even attacked in daylight, terrifying the people. The villagers sent for David, and asked him to shoot the great lion, the leader of the troop. David laid down his hammer, put on his tartan coat, picked up his rifle and followed the villager, calling to the teacher, Mebalwe, to come, too. The villagers were circling a low hill covered with bushes, and as David came up they could see the lion lying on a rock. Mebalwe lifted his rifle and took aim. The bullet hit the rock just below the lion, which snarled, pawed at the rock, and with a roar leapt up in the air, broke through the ring of villagers and made off.

David and Mebalwe turned to go back, when they saw the great lion just a few yards above them. David quickly fired both barrels of his rifle. The people shouted, "He's shot, he's shot!" but David saw that the lion was not dead, and started to load his rifle again.

As he was ramming in the bullet, he heard a shout, and looking half round, saw the lion ready to spring on him. David and the lion crashed to the ground, and the lion's jaws closed on his arm. Mebalwe quickly took aim, but his gun misfired. The lion sprang at him, and bit his thigh, and then turned on another man before it fell down dead.

*   *   *

While his arm was still healing David went

back to Kuruman to meet his old friends Dr. and Mrs. Moffat just back from Britain. He was delighted to meet them again, and to find that they had brought their twenty-three-year-old daughter, Mary, with them. They all listened to his account of the lion fight, and the building of the house at Mabotsa, and none more sympathetically than Mary. David felt himself falling in love with her, and wondered what she felt about him. She nursed him, and dressed his wounded arm and shoulder. She was friendly and happy and showed interest in his new station. He sat at night in his room at Kuruman imagining her with him at Mabotsa, and as he had watched her teaching in the school at Kuruman, and busy about her mother's house, now he saw her doing these same things with him at Mabotsa. He was sure that he loved her, and wanted her to be his wife, and he decided to ask her to marry him. One evening when they were alone in the garden he stopped her under an almond tree, and told her all that was in his heart.

They were married a year later, on January 2, 1845, at Kuruman, and the happy couple spent their honeymoon in the bullock wagon on the journey to Mabotsa.

Mary was no newcomer to Africa; she had been brought up in Kuruman, and although she had spent some years at school in England, she was able to settle down at once to the life of Mabotsa. She opened a school for the children; she made her own butter, candles and soap; and she transformed the crude brick house into a comfortable home. David used to say, "My wife is maid of all work, and I am jack of all trades."

But David was restless. He wanted to go northwards. So the great Cape wagon was loaded, and once again David set off to find a place in which to live, to teach and to preach. He and Mary travelled forty miles to the north until they came to Kolobeng, the village of chief Sechele. He was friendly, and invited them to make their home there. Once more David started to build his own house.

3

ON TO THE NORTH

FOR five years David and Mary lived in their little home at Kolobeng, and in a letter to a friend in Britain he described their life.

"We get up generally with the sun, then have family worship, breakfast and school, and as soon as these are over we begin the manual operations needed, sewing, ploughing, smithy-work, and any other sort of work by turns as required. My better half is employed all the morning in culinary and other work and feels pretty tired by dinner-time. We take about an hour of rest then, but more frequently . . . she goes off to hold infant school and this, I am happy to say, is very popular with the young-sters. My manual labour continues until five o'clock. I then go into the town to give lessons and talk to any who may be disposed for it.

As soon as the cows are milked we have a meeting—this is followed by a prayer meeting in Sechele's house, which brings me home about half-past eight and generally tired enough."

The great day came when Sechele, the chief, was baptised. David and Mary were glad, but the tribe wondered. Night after night Sechele and David talked with the headmen until they, too, came to understand that God, the Great Spirit, had come in Jesus Christ to show men and women the way He would have them live and think. This was the kind of work that David had long looked forward to, and yet he was not fully satisfied. He felt the pull of the north. He thought continually of the many thousands who lived out there beyond the horizon, who had never heard the Gospel. God was calling him to go north, and he determined to go.

One day a young chief named Lechulatabe, who lived by a great lake on the other side of the Kalahari Desert, sent a messenger asking David to come and visit him. At the same time two game hunters, Mr. Oswell and Mr.

Murray, who came to Africa every year for
their sport, were at David's home. When they
heard of the invitation they were eager to go
with him and to share their equipment and
stores. So the travellers decided to go round
the Kalahari Desert, rather than go straight
across it. They knew it was sandy waste
covered with grass and creeping plants, and in
places with trees, but there were no rivers,
only dried-up river beds, and very few springs.

Murray, Oswell and David rode on horse-
back. The going was rough, and often the Cape
wagons with their baggage sank in the soft,
light coloured sand. There were days when
there was no water, and on one occasion the
oxen were without any for four whole days.

They came at last to the banks of the beautiful
river Zouga. The people there told them that
the river came from Lake Ngami, so that all
they had to do was to follow the river to the
lake. This was simple after the desert journey,
and the caravan lumbered along the thickly
wooded banks. They came across a tribe who
lived in their dug-out canoes. They even

20

cooked their meals in them, and slept in them too. When David asked them why they lived like this they replied, "On land you have lions, serpents, hyenas, and your enemies, but in a canoe behind a bank of reeds nothing can harm you." Pushing on by canoe with these friendly river people paddling them upstream, the party passed a large tributary flowing into the main river, and the natives told them that it came from a country full of rivers. "So many that no one can tell their numbers, and full of large trees."

All this fired David's imagination. A country to the north, full of rivers, not only desert as everybody supposed! A country to explore by boat! A country full of people to hear the Gospel! He was eager to explore this unknown country.

At last they reached the north-east end of the Lake Ngami on August 1, 1849—the first Europeans ever to see it. The people told them it took three days to go round it, which they calculated would make it seventy miles in circumference. David wanted to go on to the north to see what this new country was like, and Oswell and Murray agreed. But the chief, Lechulatabe, who had invited them to come, did not wish them to move on, and refused to lend his canoes for he was an enemy of the great chief Sebituane, who lived two hundred miles to the north.

So they returned along the edge of the Kalahari to Kolobeng, where Mary and the children were waiting. There was much excitement as the travellers told their tales of the desert, the rivers and lakes, and David sent off a full report to London.

David and Mary then decided that with their children they would make another attempt to reach Sebituane's country. They set off the next year, 1850. The children thought it was great fun, and Ma Robert (as the Africans called Mary) was happy to be going with her husband. The children enjoyed their caravan holiday, with camp fires at night and with plenty of animals to see in the day-time, zebras, antelopes and elephants, and even lions. At last they arrived at the great river and were greeted by the friendly river people and enjoyed being canoed up the river, while their house on wheels made its way more slowly along the banks. "Daddy's lake," as the children called it, was a long way up the river, but when they got there they felt as if they owned it, and all the family went paddling.

But once again the chief was not friendly, So back to Kolobeng the family trekked to prepare for another attempt to go north.

There David's friend, Mr. Oswell, had prepared the caravan, and equipped it well for the journey, and early in 1851 the family once again set out to cross the Kalahari Desert. In order that there should be no shortage of water, Oswell had sent a party on ahead to dig out the water holes, and prepare the way. All went well until their guide lost his direction. They could not find any water holes, and soon the whole caravan was parched with thirst. The oxen lowed pitifully, but the children suffered most. They cried for water, and their mother had none to give them. Their tongues and their lips began to swell as they lay on the floor of the great Cape wagon. David himself was distressed for the children's sake, and there was nothing he could do but press forward.

For four days they endured agony, and David looked at his wife and children and wished that they would blame him for bringing this suffering on them. But Mary never uttered a single word of complaint. On the afternoon of the fifth day a scout came running back calling out, "Water, water." He brought a little with him, enough to save their lives. Soon they all had enough to drink, and the pots were filled. This journey was no happy camping holiday; mosquitoes bit them all until there was hardly an inch of their skin that was not punctured; the cattle died one after the other; it was with great thankfulness and relief that they reached the Chouga river.

This time they did not go up to the Lake, but sailed up the wide tributary which the river people told them would bring them to Chief Sebituane. He was a warrior chief who could run faster than any other man in his kingdom, and he was a ruthless fighter. Before

a fight he would fondle the edge of his axe,
or spear, and say, "It is sharp, and it will cut
in two any of you who run away from the
enemy." He had heard the tales of the white
men, and he wanted to make friends with them.
He went with David to choose a site for a
house, and he promised to look after Mary and
the children while the men went on to explore
the country.

One day they came to a great river. It was
the dry season. But even so the mighty stream
was three hundred to six hundred yards wide,
as it rolled on through the hot, dry country.
This, David thought, must be the great waterway the people speak about—the Zambezi.
This river, he believed, was the key to the heart
of Africa.

Not far away from the great river he saw
men and women and children being sold into
slavery. They were bartered for guns and for
cloth, as the Arab traders penetrated along the
river. He was horrified as he made his way
back to Mary and the children. How could he
best fight the slave trade? The Africans wanted

guns and cloth, and the slave traders were the only people to supply them. To fight the slave trade would mean opening up Africa to "Christianity and Commerce". So Livingstone's great idea was born. From that moment onwards he devoted his life to bringing it about. He decided to explore the great Zambezi, and then to try to find a way through to the coast, on the east or the west, in order to make a highway into Central Africa.

Mary and David talked over their plans for the future. They agreed that Mary should take the children back to England and wait there until David had made the great trail through the heart of Africa. Then he would come and bring them back. He thought he would be away for two years.

Mary and the children sailed for England on April 23, 1852. It was an unhappy day for David. They waved good-bye, Robert and Agnes and Thomas in their new clothes, and the baby, William Oswell, named after their best friend, in his mother's arms. David turned back into Cape Town and into Africa.

"I will open a path through the country," he wrote, "or perish. So powerfully am I convinced that it is the will of God that I should go that I will go, no matter who opposes."

4

THE FIRST GREAT TRAIL

DAVID LIVINGSTONE was just forty years old, and he felt that all his past experience had been preparing him for this great adventure. He was strong and fit, and he knew how to deal with the Africans so that they trusted and helped him. He was convinced that God had chosen him to open up Africa to Christianity and Commerce, and to abolish the slave trade.

As he walked, or jogged along on the back of an ox, he was continually on the alert, his keen observant eye missed nothing. He carried little black notebooks and in these he made his jottings during the day. In some of them he drew rough sketches of the country and the course of the rivers. At night before he slept he made fuller notes and wrote up his diary.

Then he turned to another little black book that he always carried, and read the Bible.

He crossed the Kalahari desert without difficulty, but when he reached the Chobe he found the river in flood, and all the country round about was a squelching bog. In his wagon he carried a light pontoon. He loaded it with food and a blanket and set off with a native companion to find a ford across which the wagons and oxen could be driven. They forced their way through the reeds and sharp-edged grass. Their clothing was cut to shreds, and their hands were bleeding, but they made a way through. They spent the night in a deserted hut, and the next day paddled down the river till sunset, when they spotted a village on the north bank. The villagers couldn't believe their eyes. This was a village David had visited on his earlier journey, so they knew him, but that he should arrive without their knowing it astounded them. They said, "He must have dropped among us from the clouds, yet came riding upon an hippopotamus. We Makololo thought no one could cross the Chobe without our knowledge, but here he drops like a bird."

Pushing on to Linyanti the court herald came out to greet them. He stood up and roared out, "Don't I see the white man? Don't I see the comrade of Sebituane? Don't I see the father of Sekeletu? Give thy son sleep, my lord."

Sebituane had died and the young Sekeletu was now chief. One night he came to David's hut, and said, "Tell me what you want from me." David replied, "I have come only to help your people and to make them Christians." Sekeletu said, "I do not wish to read the 'Book', for it may make me change my ways, and have only one wife. I want to have five wives at least. But is there nothing that you want from me?"

"I will be pleased to accept one of your canoes, but nothing else," said David. "I have not come to get, but to give."

"You must accept these ten tusks of ivory. They are my present to you. I insist."

"I do not accept presents for myself, but if I must take them," said David, "please understand that I will use them to help you. I have brought you some presents, too, from the south, some goats, and some chickens, and two cats. They are good and big. Will you take them to improve your stock?"

"Thank you very much. They will be well used by my people, for these are finer than any we have."

Then the chief formed a royal party to accompany David to the upper parts of the river to find high ground on which he might build a mission station, and to which he could bring his family. At every village the people brought large pots of beer and pots of thick milk, which were distributed among the royal party. Each night there was a festival dance, and feasting on roast ox. But failing to find any place in which it would be suitable for Europeans to live, David decided to put the second part of his plan into action: to open up a trail to Loanda fifteen hundred miles away on the west coast.

Most of the Makololo people were in favour of helping David reach the coast, and they agreed to send twenty-seven men with him.

It was made clear that he was not hiring them, but that they were going with him because their people wanted to open up a path to the coast as much as he did. There was one question left. "If you die will not the white people blame us?" David replied, "No, because I will leave a book with Sekeletu, in which I will explain all that has happened."

He made his baggage fit into four tin boxes. One contained shirts, trousers and shoes to be used when they reached civilisation; the second medicines; the third, books, a nautical almanac, logarithm tables and a Bible; the fourth a magic lantern. The sextant, thermometer, compasses, artificial horizon, were carried separately, so were beads for barter, tea, sugar, coffee and biscuits. In addition, he had a small gipsy tent, a sheepskin blanket, and a horse rug, three muskets for his people, and a rifle and double-barrelled smooth bore for himself. With shouts and yells from the oarsmen and their friends the canoes shot down the Chobe on November 11, 1853.

The canoes made their way up the Zambezi,

often oppressed by the heat, and troubled by rocks and rapids, but always moving on. The oarsmen stood while they rowed, and shouted to each other from boat to boat. They made each day's rowing a boat race. In his journal David describes the daily routine.

"We get up a little before 5 a.m.; it is then beginning to dawn. While I am dressing, coffee is made, and having filled my pannikin, the rest is handed round to my companions who relish it greatly. The next two hours are the most pleasant of the day's sail. The men paddle vigorously . . . About eleven we land and eat any meat that may have remained over from the previous evening's meal, or a biscuit, with honey and drink water. After an hour we again embark and cower under an umbrella. The heat is oppressive. The men being quite uncovered in the sun perspire freely. . . . Sometimes we reach a sleeping place two hours before sunset, and we gladly remain for the night. Coffee again and a biscuit and a piece of coarse bread made of maize meal, or that of native corn, make up the bill of fare for the

evening, unless we have been fortunate enough
to kill something, then we boil a potful of flesh.
That is done by cutting it up into long strips
and pouring on water until it is covered. When
that is boiled dry the meat is considered ready."

At night the men collected grass for their
leader's bed, and arranged the boxes on either
side of it. They covered the grass with his
horse rug, and laid his sheepskin rug on top
of that, for him to use as a blanket. Next they
built the main camp fire. The men then
arranged themselves around the fire, each
according to his rank. When they slept the
head boat man made his bed at the door of
David's tent, as soon as he retired. The rest
divided into small groups according to their
tribes, in a big horseshoe round the fire, and
inside the horseshoe they drove the oxen.

David ate the same food as his companions,
native food cooked in native style. He taught
one of them to wash his shirts and socks, and
in the midst of that tropical jungle he kept
himself clean and tidy. He changed his clothes
very frequently, and made sure that his sleep-

ing blanket was sunned every day to keep it fresh and free from bugs. His personal habits, his regular routine, his camp-fire prayers, his private devotions, his daily writing, and consistent observation made its impression on his primitive companions. They honoured him as they did their own chief, and trusted him with their lives.

One evening he was showing magic-lantern pictures of Abraham about to kill his son, Isaac, and the chief and his wives were sitting at the front near the sheet which he had fixed up for a screen. He told them the story, and pointed to the large knife in Abraham's hand with which he was about to strike his boy. Then he moved the slide off the screen, and the ladies screamed in terror, shouting, "Mother, mother," and rushed off helter skelter, knocking over their idol huts in their fear. The talk had to stop, and David was told that as he moved the slide the dagger came towards them, and they thought it was going to stick in them. Nothing could persuade them to come back.

On January 6, 1857, they reached a

village which was ruled by a chieftainess. David tried to explain what he was doing in her country, but she was not friendly, because the Makololo were her enemies. So David spoke out, "I bring you a message of Peace, from one no less than God, who made heaven and earth, and all that is therein. If the Makololo break His laws again and attack you, the guilt will rest on them alone. He would have you live at peace with one another, and with all men. He made us all, He is our Father, your Father, and my Father."

"That cannot be," she replied, "for you are not like us. Your hair is not hair at all, it is like the mane of a lion."

"My hair is just like yours, only yours has been frizzled in the sun," said David. "It is the same with my skin. Look at my hands and my face, they are almost as dark as yours, because they have been scorched in the sun. But look now at my chest, which is white, because it has been protected from the sun by my shirt." Then they agreed that he and they belonged to the same God.

At one village on the main slave route to the coast David's party had already sent the chief a present of the hump and ribs of an ox that they had killed, but he sent back a messenger saying, "Our chief is a great man, you must give to him a present of a man, or a gun, or an ox, or gunpowder, or cloth or a shell, and if you do not he will not allow you to pass through his district."

David replied, "No chief ought to demand tribute on a party that was merely passing through, and not dealing in slaves, and I do not intend to give your chief any more than I have already given him."

"But the slave traders always give us a man, and others give us cloth; you must give."

"Tell me," asked David, "what crime have we committed that you should come to us armed and ready to fight?"

The chief replied, "This morning one of your men spat at one of my messengers, and for this guilt, you must pay with a man, an ox, or a gun."

"Is this true?" asked David. "Yes," volunteered Pitsane, "but it was an accident. I had just given the man a piece of meat, which he had accepted. Then as I was spitting some fell on his leg, which at once I wiped off with my hand."

"That is so," said the chief, "but you must pay as I have said."

"I would rather die than give you a man to be your slave," retorted David. "These are free men, we are all free men. You can ask them to give me to you for they have as much right to do that as I have to give one of them."

"Then you can give us one of your guns," insisted the chief.

"Do you think I am going to give you one of my guns when you have come here to plunder our goods?"

"We have not come to plunder. All we ask is that you pay the tribute for passing through our land."

"Is the land yours?" asked David, who knew their customs. "Is the land not God's, who is your Father, and my Father? I do not have to pay for walking on my Father's ground."

"That is so," admitted the chief, "but for the insult of spitting you must pay."

David's men gathered round their leader, and entreated him to give something.

"Very well," said David, "I will give you one of my shirts. Here it is."

"That is not enough," shouted the chief. His warriors were restive, and waved their swords. Pitsane said, "Please give them more as it was my fault."

"I will add a bunch of beads then."

"That is still not enough," the headman shrieked, "give more." The native warriors were moving in and out, beating their feet and shouting. One of them rushed at David from behind, but he turned round quickly and pushed the muzzle of his gun to the man's mouth. He moved back quickly.

"I do not want to fight you," said David, "but if you will not let us pass quietly you must strike the first blow. You must know that you are guilty of our blood before God."

They said nothing. He said nothing. So they sat, with David in the centre of that savage scene. He was cool and ready. At last the chief spoke, "You come among us in a new way and say that you are quite friendly. How can we know it unless you give us some of your food and you take some of ours? If you give us an ox we will give you whatever you wish, and then we shall be friends."

David's men begged him to give the ox they asked, and as there seemed to be no other way out without bloodshed he agreed.

"I will give you an ox, and you can bring to me some fowl, and some meal."

So the peace was kept. That evening the messengers returned bringing their gifts. They brought a small basket of meal, and a few pounds of the ox flesh which they had been given. They apologised, and said, "We have no fowls, and very little food at all. This is all we can give."

As they were now going through well-beaten narrow forest tracks, David rode on one of the oxen. He found that the one he named Sinbad had the softest back, but also a hasty temper, and he seemed to delight in trying to knock

David off his back by dashing under low lying branches. Once when they were crossing a river Sinbad rushed in and tossed his rider into the water.

The forest was gloomy and oppressively hot, and the tribes were unfriendly. The stores were running out, and they had little left to barter, or for gifts, and each tribe demanded more than the last. The Makololo men wanted to go back. They said they were tired and could not go any further, that they were afraid, and must go back. David heard their complaints with a heavy heart. He, too, was weary, but he was determined to get through. They were on the edge of the Portuguese territory, and the journey was almost over.

He talked with them and tried to persuade them to go on with him, but he seemed to make little impression. In the end he said, "You do what you think right. I will go on alone." He got up and walked slowly back to his tent where he knelt down and asked God to help him. As he knelt there the head of Mohorisi appeared through the door of the tent, and as if in answer to his prayer he said, "Do not be unhappy. We will never leave you. Wherever you lead we will follow." The others followed one by one. They said, "Be comforted. You are our father, we are your children. You and Sekeletu are our chiefs. We will die for you."

The rain was almost ceaseless. Everything they carried was wet through. David's clothes and rugs were mouldy and the only place he could find to keep his watch dry was underneath his armpit. His tent was rotted and the rain had softened his men's feet. He was weak through repeated attacks of fever and dysentery, but he kept on. He drove himself forward. He kept a record of each day's happenings, and whenever the sun came through he took readings.

At last they reached the Portuguese town of Cassange.

David and his men were a puzzle to the Portuguese authorities and traders. They thought David must be a Government agent, and they would not believe him when he said he was a missionary. "Why," they asked, "does a missionary want to calculate longitude and latitudes? Why are you a doctor? Tell us please what rank you hold in the British army."

"I am an ordinary missionary of the Gospel. I am also a doctor, so that I can help the suffering people. My reason for coming here is to find a path through to the coast from the centre of Africa, along which trade may flow, and missionaries may come. I hope that this will result in the ending of the slave trade, too, although I know that you gentlemen find that a very profitable trade."

It was another three hundred miles to the coast. During this march David was so ill that he could not hold his instruments steady for taking observations, nor do the simple calculations needed. He forgot the days of the week, the names of his companions, and even doubted if he could remember his own name. His companions were full of fears about Loanda, the town to which they were going. They came and asked him, "Father, what will happen to us in the great town? Will we be

separated from each other? May we not be
kidnapped and sold as slaves?" He replied,
"I am as ignorant of Loanda as you are, but
nothing will happen to you that does not happen
to me."

The first sight of the sea, stretching in
sparkling blueness to the distant horizon, filled
his men with awe. They were silent. Then
one of them said, "We marched along with
our Father, believing that what the ancients
had always told us was true, that the world
had no end. But all at once the world said
to us: 'I am finished; there is no more of
me.' "

There was only one Englishman in Loanda,
and he was so shocked to see David looking
so ill, that at once he offered him his own bed.
David ever remembered the luxury and the
joy of that moment when he lay on a bed again
after six months of sleeping on the ground.
And so, on May 31, 1854, the first great
trail was over.

5

FROM WEST TO EAST

DAVID stayed for four months in Loanda. Gradually his health was restored. The surgeon of the frigate, *Polyphemus*, which was lying off Loanda in the slave trade blockade, looked after him, and the Captain of the ship tried to persuade him to return to England. There was nothing that he was longing for more than to see Mary and the children, and to be cared for by them, but even in his weak state he did not hesitate. "I have given my word to my companions to take them back home," he said, and he got ready for the march eastwards.

Meanwhile his men were thoroughly enjoying the town. They gaped at the houses in bewilderment, and described them as "mountains with caves in them". They were taken on board the frigate which to them was not a canoe but a "town to which you had to climb on a rope". They worked for part of the time on the water front unloading coal for sixpence a day. Describing it later to their own people in Linyanti, they said, "We worked from the rising till the setting sun for a moon and a half (six weeks), taking out stones that burn. We were tired, but there was still plenty left in the ship." Their greatest thrill came when they were given by the Bishop of Loanda, who was the acting Governor, special uniforms of blue and red cloth, and for their chief, Sekeletu, a colonel's uniform and a horse.

The merchants of Loanda presented them with many samples of their goods, and also two donkeys on which to carry them. The sailors made David a new tent, and he was able to buy all the ammunition he wanted. He gave each of his men a musket which they carried very proudly on all occasions.

He set off on September 20, 1854. The rain fell in torrents, drenching everything they possessed. As they climbed out of Cassange

valley David was attacked by rheumatic fever.
It was brought on, he says, by having to sleep
on a plain covered with water. As soon as he
felt a little better he wanted to move on, but
his men insisted that he waited. The headman
of the village where he was lying ill had been
bargaining for a piece of meat and had lost his
temper. One of David's men struck him across
the mouth. He demanded payment for the
insult of a "blow on the beard". They gave
him a gun and five pieces of cloth, but that
did not satisfy him. He sent to the surrounding
villages for help. It was clear that he would
demand more and more, so David gave the
order to move on.

His men set out in a long thin line, each
with his load on his head, as they wended their
way along the narrow foot track of the forest.
Suddenly they heard shots being fired. The
man at the end of the file had been knocked
down. David staggered to the front of the
caravan grasping his six barrelled revolver, and
there faced the offended chief. David glared
at him and pointed the revolver at his naked

stomach. The chief cried out, "Oh, I have only come to speak to you and wish you peace only." David could see the man trembling with fear, and when he examined his gun he saw that it had been fired.

Both parties now closed in behind their chiefs, and the situation was becoming difficult. David kept calm.

"Everybody sit down," he shouted. Turning to the chief he said, "If you have come with peaceful intentions, we have no other. Go away home to your village."

"I am afraid lest you shoot me in the back," replied the chief.

"If I wanted to kill you I could shoot you in the face as well; look, I am not afraid of you," and David stood up, turned round and walked slowly back to his ox.

At the rate of two miles an hour, David led his men along the track eastwards. Some of the villages off the main trade tracks were very friendly, and wanted them to stay for a day or so.

In one of them the people said, "We will

not give you a guide unless you stay with us for a day."

At another, the chief demanded an ox before he would ferry them over the river, and paddled his canoes to the other side to show them that he meant business. Pitsane took careful note of the place where they were tied up, and during the night he swam over and paddled a load back. Quietly in the darkness the whole party was taken over, and the canoe returned to its hiding place.

At the town of Libonta there were great rejoicings. The women danced and sang their "lulliloos", they kissed the hands and cheeks of their friends, and the whole town turned out to meet them. When they settled down in their town meeting, Pitsane addressed them. He spoke for an hour and described the high spots of the journey, the wonders of Loanda, the friendship of David. "He has done more for us than we had expected. Not only has he opened up a path for us to the other white men, but he has made friends with all the chiefs along the route. He is our Father."

David's men dressed themselves up in their uniforms, and their red caps, and marched as they had seen the soldiers marching in Loanda, with their guns over their shoulders. They were the pride and wonder of the town. David spoke to the people about the goodness of God in preserving them from the dangers of strange tribes and animals. Alone in that African jungle, surrounded by hundreds of excited people, he reminded them that God had guarded them on that journey.

And so they arrived back in Linyanti on September 11, 1855. They had been away for two years. A great meeting was held, and David's men said, "We walked until we had finished the whole world, and we only turned back when there was no more land."

For two months he rested in Linyanti. He spent his time writing up his journal. In the evenings he gathered the people together and spoke to them with the aid of his lantern, teaching them the Bible stories.

*　　*　　*

In David's mind was the question, "What about the road to the east?" He was determined to find the answer. An Arab trader told him of a large inland sea and great rivers. "The chiefs," said the Arab, "are friendly. They will let you pass through their country."

"Surely this must be the way," thought David, "to the east there is a way into Central Africa." He decided to go, and Sekeletu promised to provide another party of men to go with him.

On November 3, 1855, with Sekeletu and about two hundred of his men, thirteen oxen for riding and for food, and a quantity of ivory for trading, David set out. He was entirely dependent on the generosity of Sekeletu, for all his own goods and money had been used. The young chief loved him and did everything he could to help him. One night David and Sekeletu had sent most of the men on ahead to prepare the camp, while they waited behind with the oxen. The night turned into a tropical storm. Lightning lit up the sky in blinding flashes, and the thunder was frighteningly loud: the rain lashed down. They had to give up any attempt to reach their camp, and wet to the skin they turned aside to a fire they saw in the distance, which had been made by some other party of travellers. Without tent or blanket David lay down in the wet grass to sleep. Sekeletu came up and covered him with his own blanket. "You take my blanket, my Father," he said.

Down the Chobe river to the mighty Zambezi! Some sailed in canoes and others drove the oxen along the banks.

David had heard of the great waterfall, called the Sounding Smoke, and now he was near enough to visit it. He was paddled down the river in a canoe by men who knew the river well. Five miles away he could see great columns of what looked like smoke rising high into the sky and blending with the clouds. He watched the wind driving the misty vapour. The columns were white at the bottom and seemed to become darker as they went higher, as though some huge tract of grass were on fire.

About half a mile from the falls the party changed into a lighter canoe, and paddled carefully down the centre of the stream to a small island on the very edge of the falls. David crept forward and gazed down into the vast chasm of raging water. The great river, over a mile broad at this point, poured itself into a great crack in the earth and seemed to disappear. Only eighty feet away from where he lay on the lip of the falls he could see the other side of the great crack in the earth's surface.

As he peered down through the clouds of ascending vapour, he saw the water churning in great cascades about three hundred feet below, and then rushing through a narrow gorge no more than fifteen or twenty yards wide. From this seething cauldron the vapour rose like a jet of steam far into the sky, and fell again in a constant shower of rain. As he lay looking at this wonder of the world David knew he was the first white man to see it. He gave it the Queen's name—the Victoria Falls.

The air now was cooler. At 6 a.m. it was seventy degrees, at midday ninety degrees, and in the evening eighty-four degrees. Up and up the party climbed until they came to the top of a ridge. David estimated the height as five thousand feet, because he noted that water boiled there at two hundred and two degrees. These ridges and uplands were healthier than any he had seen in his trek. As he sat writing in his diary, looking over the beautiful wooded and grassy slopes, listening to the little honey bird pleading to be allowed to show him where he might find honey, watching the wild animals peacefully grazing, he thought he saw thriving British farms with cows and sheep grazing on the rich pasture and a mission station with its schools and church, and happy, laughing children.

They pressed on to the coast, and soon came to the borders of the Portuguese territory. The natives here were not friendly, and when David asked for canoes to ferry his party across the wide Loangwa river they lent him two only. He was suspicious, and could see that they intended to attack when they had divided his party. Large numbers of armed warriors appeared and there were no women.

He decided to cross during the night. He took evening prayers with his men, and he must have read the last verses of St. Matthew's Gospel to them, for when he returned to his tent he made an entry in his diary. He wrote, "Felt some turmoil of spirit at having all my efforts for the welfare of this great region and its teeming population knocked on the head by savages to-morrow. But I read that Jesus came and said, 'All power is given unto me in heaven and earth. Lo, I am with you always, even unto the end of the world.'" He underlined these words with his pencil, and then went on to write, "It is the word of a gentleman of the most sacred and strictest honour, and there's an end on't. I will not cross furtively by night as I had intended. I shall take observations for latitude and longitude to-night, though they be my last. I feel calm now, thank God."

The next morning, the armed natives lent

them only one canoe, although there were two others tied up to the bank. The river was a mile wide, and David sent over first his goods, then his cattle and men. While they were crossing he took out his magnifying glass, and fascinated the savage warriors by making dried leaves burn. He held up his watch and let them listen to it ticking. He talked with them all the time, and assured them that he wanted peace. All his party were safely over. He said good-bye, and stepped into the waiting canoe, which was paddled away into mid-stream. The natives on the bank made no move to shoot or throw a spear. Once more David Livingstone had succeeded in making friends with a hostile people.

On the night of March 2, 1856, he arrived within eight miles of Tete. He couldn't walk any further that day, so he sent a messenger on ahead with his letters of introduction to the commandant of Tete. At two o'clock in the morning the whole camp was disturbed by the arrival of two Portuguese officers and a company of soldiers. They had come to welcome

Dr. Livingstone and had brought food with them for his breakfast.

The Portuguese lent him a boat, and he sailed downstream on the great Zambezi river. "This is the waterway," he said to himself. "This is what I have been looking for. A steamer could sail right up here from the coast. Then there are the highland ridges for Europeans to live on. Yes, this is it. I will come back and open up this area to Christianity and Commerce. My journeys have not been in vain. Thanks be to God." Two months later he reached the coast of Quilimane. His four years of trail making in Africa were over. He sailed for home at last.

David could hardly believe the enthusiastic welcome which he received in Britain. Large public meetings were held to honour him. Queen Victoria sent for him, and he amused her by telling her that often in Africa the people had asked him about his chief, and their first question always was "How many cows has she?" He was made a Freeman of the City of London, and of the City of Glasgow, and Glasgow also gave him £2,000. Universities honoured him with degrees, and he was greeted in the streets as he walked about. He was the most famous man of his day.

One day in Cambridge he ended an address to undergraduates with these words, "Gentlemen, I direct your attention to Africa. I know that in a few years I shall be cut off in that country which is now open. I go back to try to open up a path to Commerce and Christianity. Do you carry on the work that I have begun. I leave it to you."

Within a few months he was back again on the Zambezi to lead an expedition for the Government.

6

SLAVES ON THE ZAMBEZI

DAVID LIVINGSTONE and his party set out from England on March 10, 1858, in H.M.S. *Pearl*. Mary sailed with them, but she disembarked at Cape Town, and went up to Kuruman to stay with her parents. With him in this Government expedition were six other British members, each of whom had a special task. The most outstanding of these men was Dr. Kirk, who was botanist and doctor. David's brother, Charles, was photographer and general assistant; there was Commander Bedingfield the navigator, and Richard Thornton as geologist, and George Rae an engineer from Blantyre, whose task it was to care for the river boats.

The expedition was equipped with a specially built river steamer, which was carried in sections on the *Pearl*. When they reached Zanzibar the sailors riveted and screwed the boat together. David was sure that he could find a river which was navigable, and which would carry him right into the heart of Africa. She was made out of a new light steel, and was a wood burning steamer, seventy feet long, and driven by paddles. There was sleeping accommodation for members of the party, and the deck space was covered with an awning for protection from the sun.

David christened her the *Ma Robert*, Mary's African name, but before long he was to call her many other names, the chief of which was the "Old Asthmatic", "with engines fit only to grind coffee in a shop window." The special steel soon corroded, and became full of holes which had to be bunged with clay. The wood took two days to cut and was used up in one day. She was not easy to steer, and frequently ran into sand banks which grounded her for hours at a time. It was little wonder that Commander Bedingfield resigned after only a few months, yet it was in the "Old Asthmatic" that the expedition sailed for thousands of miles, most of which David himself navigated, though, as he said, he would far sooner have been driving a cab in a November fog in London.

The first part of the river voyage up the Zambezi was in grand style with the *Pearl* steaming ahead of the *Ma Robert*. They made Tete the headquarters of the expedition, and set out to try and find a passage up the Zambezi. The Kebrabasa Rapids looked impassable. David and his party sailed up the river, anchored the *Ma Robert* at the foot of the rapids, and went overland to examine them. Clambering from rock to rock, in places they had to wriggle round large protruding boulders which hung over the swirling waters of the rapids below. They were torn and bleeding in the thick thorn undergrowth, and they were only able to travel about one mile an hour. "Our feet are in lumps," said the porters, "our flesh is torn, and still he goes on. He is going where no foot has ever been, where there is no way. He is mad. We will not go further." Dr. Kirk did not understand the language and David had to translate for him. With three of the Makololo they went on until they had explored the whole fifty miles of the rapids, and of a further cataract beyond. They saw that the river was jammed between two mountains with perpendicular sides, and that it was less than fifty yards wide.

Three times he returned to the Kebrabasa rapids. He concluded that if they were to force a way through it would have to be during the flood season, and for this they would need a much more powerful vessel than the *Ma Robert*, so he sent a request home for a more suitable vessel.

Next he turned to the River Shire, a northern tributary of the Zambezi. The "Old Asthmatic" puffed her way through the duckweed, and the crew kept a sharp look-out on the banks where they could see crowds of natives excitedly fingering their bows and arrows. As they sailed up to a village they saw about five hundred natives on the shore. David stopped the ship and jumped into the river and walked slowly ashore. He called to them, "We are English. We have come with peace. We do not wish to fight. We are not after slaves. We want to be friends with you. Let us exchange goods with one another." They listened to this brave man who explained his mission as he walked towards them. They knew that at any moment they could shoot him down, but their chief, Tingane, gave no order. David asked him to call his people together that they might talk. The tall elderly chief gave the command, and the people gathered around him.

They all sat down and David spoke to them. "We are British, and you know that our ships are sailing the seas to stop the slave traffic." They grunted their approval. "We have come to you," he went on, "to help you. We want you to grow cotton, which you can sell, and that is far better than selling your own brothers and sisters. We believe there is only one God, who has made all things and who is Chief over all people. We want to teach you about Him. We have a book which tells about Him. We all belong to Him, and He wants you to know Him."

They accepted his word, and he parted from

them their friend. They sailed up stream, and every few yards they took soundings. The river got gradually shallower, until they could go no further.

They returned again to Tete, for the wet season was starting. While they waited for three months they collected stores from the coast. In the middle of March 1859 they set off again up the Shire. The chiefs were friendly, and apart from the leaking "Asthmatic" the journey was pleasant. They left their ship and set off to explore to the north. As they climbed they heard the steady beat of drums as the natives passed on the news of this small party making for the mountains. The tribes were less and less friendly, and the climb was increasingly difficult. In fourteen days they covered only forty miles. David would not turn back and on April 18 they came to Lake Shirwa. The water was bitter, but there were fish, crocodiles, hippopotami in abundance. The country round about was mountainous and healthy. This lake, he estimated, was between sixty and eighty miles wide, and the natives told him that further into the mountain range was an even bigger lake.

He returned to Tete to gather a larger company of men. Here was the place where Europeans could live without fear of fever and he could hardly wait to find out more about it. He took with him thirty-six Makololo, two guides, and three other Europeans. They left the ship on August 18, 1859, and were soon enjoying the beauty of Nyasaland. On the mountains they slept under the trees, and loved the cool, fresh air. They climbed up the Shire valley into the beautiful hill country, and on September 16 saw Lake Nyasa. David sat thinking about the slave trade as he gazed down on the beautiful lake, and wondered if with a steamer plying to and fro on the lake and down the Shire to the rapids he could stamp out this trade?

He argued that it was only the ivory that the slaves carried that made it worth while their drivers taking them down to the coast, for it cost more to feed them than they actually fetched on the slave market. If, therefore, a small trading vessel could be placed on the lake it would quickly and easily make the slave trade unprofitable. He discussed it with his colleagues and they agreed, so he ordered a ship to be built in Glasgow at his own expense. As he led his party back down the Shire they talked and planned about opening up this district. It would be an ideal place, they thought, to which to bring a colony of people from Britain, who would settle down and make their home there, bringing with them their agriculture, simple industries, and their faith.

Then from Tete northwards the route led past the Victoria Falls once more. The two men (Livingstone and Kirk) measured the depth of the rift by lowering a line over the edge. Lying flat at the edge of this deafening cascade of water David paid out a line on to the end of which he had tied a piece of white cotton cloth and a few bullets for weight. At 310 feet the weight rested on a ledge, fifty feet above the surface of the water. He then measured the distance across the rift with his sextant and found it to be eighty yards at its narrowest. Into this slot in the earth's surface they watched the great Zambezi, with its 1860 yards of water, tumble with an incredible roar, sending its columns of spray into the sky.

On the return journey they tried to sail on the Zambezi from below the Victoria Falls. With two of Sekeletu's men in two canoes they had a fearful journey. Rapids, whirlpools, hidden rocks and dangerous currents all combined to break up the canoes. Dr. Kirk's canoe was smashed in pieces and he lost all his notes and specimens. He only just managed to escape from being sucked down into a gigantic whirlpool.

Once more they boarded the *Ma Robert*. David wrote, "It was hard to keep the vessel afloat; we never expected her to remain above water. New leaks broke out every day; the engine pump gave way; the bridge broke down; three compartments filled at night; and in a few days we were assured by Rowe that 'she can't be worse than she is.' The morning of the 21 December the uncomfortable 'Asthmatic' grounded on a sandbank and filled. She could neither be emptied nor got off. The river rose during the night, and all that was visible of the worn-out craft next day was about six feet of her two masts, and we spent the Christmas of 1860 encamped on the island of Chimba."

About the same time the Universities' Mission sent out its first missionaries, and David gave himself to the task of taking Bishop Mackenzie and his party to the Shire highlands. He enjoyed their company, and they spent hours discussing the possibilities of the mission. One of the main problems was the slave traffic. How should they tackle it? They all agreed with his policy of driving it out by fair trade. But what about the hundreds of slaves who were marching and dying daily? One afternoon, the village chief came up and said, "In a little while a slave gang will pass through my village."

"What are we going to do?" David asked. "Shall we interfere and free the slaves?"

"If you do that," one of the party said, "then

all our goods at Tete may be taken by the Portuguese."

"This is different," said David, "the slave traders never dared to come up the Shire until we came. Now they are going to villages and saying that they are 'our children'. They are making the tribes fight one another. They are undoing all the good that we are trying to do."

A long line of manacled men, women and children, driven forward by muskets and whips, came down the trail. When the drivers saw the English party they fled. The slaves knelt down and clapped their hands to show their gratitude, and soon the women and children were freed. The men had to be sawn free, as each of them was fastened around the neck with the fork of a thick stick, six or seven feet long, and secured by an iron rod which was riveted at both ends. The slaves could hardly believe they were free. One little boy said, "The others tied and starved us. You cut the ropes and tell us to eat. What sort of people are you? Where do you come from?"

They decided that the freed slaves should be allowed to return to their homes, but the slaves said, "We want to stay with you. You will look after us." The Bishop then agreed that they could become part of the mission, and that with these freed slaves he could begin his work. So together the party trudged on to Lake Nyasa.

Village after village round the lake was burnt to the ground. One place where David had seen people quietly weaving cloth on his previous visit was now burnt out. The harvests were rotting in the fields, and in the distance they could see the smoke rising from more burning houses. They could hear the distant wail of the women lamenting their dead. Bishop Mackenzie called the party to pray, and they knelt in the rough grass as he called upon God to guide and direct them.

When they arose from their knees they saw a long line of warriors with their captives coming towards them. David called to them. "We have come to talk to you. We want to speak to your chief." Unfortunately, some of the natives who were with him were over-excited, and they shouted, "Our Chibisa is come." Chibisa was well known as a great fighter, and the Ajawa warriors, hearing the name Chibisa, ran off screaming and yelling, "Nkondo! Nkondo!" (War! War!)

Soon large numbers of warriors appeared all round the missionary party. Bows and arrows, spears and javelins, could be seen in the long grass and waving behind huge boulders. Suddenly there was a shower of arrows. One carrier was hit in the arm. The missionary party slowly retreated up the hill, and this made the enemy more eager. They came within fifty yards and four of them who had muskets fired them. David had to order his party to shoot in self-defence.

David, Dr. Kirk and Charles Livingstone went on to explore the lake. They carried with them a light, four-oared boat, and launched it on the broad smooth waters of the Upper Shire. White breasted cormorants rose in protest as they passed, and hippopotami plunged after them. One snapped his huge jaws so near to the boat that water splashed on the stern sheets.

On September 2, 1861, they sailed into Lake Nyasa.

On the shores of the lake was almost a continuous line of villages. David had never seen so many people living together in Africa. They took a great interest in the party of explorers, and wherever they went crowds watched them. At meal times they had to draw a line on the sand and tell the people that they must not come nearer than that. The lake teemed with fish, which was good to eat; the lakeside country was fertile, and the climate was healthy. Again David longed for an English colony to live here. He longed all the more as he saw an Arab dhow filled with slaves plying to and fro across the lake, and as he climbed the various hills around and came across village after village which had been razed to the ground by marauders. He reckoned that about two hundred thousand people were victims of the slave traffic from the Nyasa district alone each year. Of these only one-tenth ever reached the slave markets, the others were murdered or died of their wounds or fatigue on the forced marches.

The party returned to the *Pioneer*, their new launch, on November 8, 1861. Here they met Bishop Mackenzie. "There is peace in the highlands," he said; "the Ajawa have sent messengers saying that they want to live at peace with us, and it looks as if the slave trade is ceasing, and the people are beginning to feel free again. I hope that very soon we will be able to grow enough food to be largely self-supporting." David rejoiced to hear this. There was more good news too. Recruits were arriving. An energetic young man named Birrup, a surgeon and a lay brother had made their way up from the coast by canoe, and within a few weeks they were to be joined by Birrup's wife, the Bishop's sister and another lady. The same boat was also bringing his own Mary and for David no news could be better than this.

David set off to be in time to welcome Mary and the others at the coast. The *Pioneer*, however, was grounded in the shallow waters of the river and for five weary weeks they tried

to float her. It was an unhealthy spot, with
large marshes on both sides. The carpenter's
mate was taken ill with fever and one evening
while the ship's company were at prayers, he
died, and they buried him ashore. This was the
first death in the three and a half years the expedition had been in the country.

The delay was unfortunate for by the time
David got to the coast the ship *Gordon* had
arrived, and finding no one to meet her had
put to sea again. But soon, after nearly four
years, David and Mary were together again.

It was necessary to get the women away
from the fever-infested coast as soon as possible
and the Captain of the *Gordon* agreed to take
them up to the Shire to meet Bishop Mackenzie.
David stayed behind with Mary to superintend
the overhaul of the *Pioneer*, and the erection of
the new steamboat which he had ordered and
paid for himself to patrol Lake Nyasa. It had
come in twenty-four sections and was too heavy
for the *Pioneer* to carry. He named her *Lady
Nyasa*.

Then came news that Bishop Mackenzie and

Mr. Birrup were dead. They had set off to rescue some of their people from the slave traders, and then without proper rest they had hurried to meet the newcomers from the coast. The river was rough and they were soaked through many times. After sailing all day they tied up for the night, but were so plagued with mosquitoes that they decided to sail on in the darkness. They were caught up in a whirlpool, the canoe overturned, and they lost everything including their medicines. They managed to rescue the canoe and they lay in it all night, wet, cold and shivering. The next morning the Bishop was feverish. They had no medicine and there was nothing anyone could do for him. He fell unconscious and died. Birrup, who watched helplessly, buried him; then hurried on. He, too, was exhausted, and when he arrived he was too weak to resist the fever and he died.

David was broken-hearted. "This will hurt us all," he said, and later, after he had thought about the cost in human life of bringing the Gospel to the people of Africa, he added, "I shall not swerve a hairbreadth from my work, while life is spared."

And now came a further blow, the hardest of all. His own Mary was taken ill, and despite all his care her life slowly slipped away and she died on April 27, 1862. He buried her under a large baobab tree, and he wept bitterly. "For the first time in my life I am willing to die," he said. He sat down and wrote to each of his children, and to many of his friends, with tears running down his cheeks. "You must think of her," he wrote to his son, Oswell, "as beckoning to you from heaven." It was in this way that he always thought of her, and she was never far from his mind.

Now he had to get his own ship *Lady Nyasa* up to the lake. The *Pioneer* towed her till they came to the cataracts. Here they took her to pieces to carry her to the level of the lake. David was determined to get his steamer on to Lake Nyasa. He had to blaze a path along which the parts of the steamer could be carried, and as it meant cutting down the forest trees for forty miles, it was obviously going to take a long time. He couldn't get any help from the slave-raided villages, so with his own porters he started hacking a road through the forest. They had not gone very far before a despatch arrived from the Foreign Office in London recalling him. The expedition was over. He could do nothing but obey, though he was sadly disappointed that he had not been able to get his steamer on to the lake. It was a disappointed David who reached the coast on February 13, 1864, to be picked up by H.M.S. *Orestes*.

David now planned to sell his ship, so he was towed in it by H.M.S. *Ariel* to Mozambique. There he refused to sell her because he saw that she would be sold again to slave traders. The only other possible market was across the Indian Ocean at Bombay. He decided to sail her across that stormy sea.

The crew was three Europeans, a stoker, a sailor, and a carpenter, and seven native Zambezians, who had never seen the sea before. David himself was navigator. He reckoned that they could make the voyage in eighteen days,

but they were becalmed for days on end, and
when the engines were working she made little
headway. The days slipped by. They lay becalmed in the silent sea, surrounded by dolphins
and sharks and flying fish. "The near approach
of the monsoon period," he wrote, "in which
we believed no boat could live, made some of
us think our epitaph would be: Left Zanzibar
30 April, 1864, and never more heard of."

Then came the monsoon. The rain flooded
down. As the squalls of wind hit the little ship
she swung round and round and almost cap-
sized. David held on to the wheel, hour after
weary hour. Then they saw seaweed and
serpents floating past, and knew they must be
nearing the coast. The next day at noon they
sighted land, and crept into the harbour at
Bombay having sailed two thousand miles. No
one noticed their arrival, but when it became
known that David Livingstone had arrived he
was made guest of honour of the Governor,
and was fêted by the Bombay merchants. He
reached London in July 1864.

David was happy again with his children.

Agnes was now sixteen and very proud of her father. Thomas and Oswell were growing up, and there was little Anna Mary who had never seen her father before. He gathered them all around him, and told them exciting stories of Africa and he played with them by the hour. He greatly missed Robert, his eldest boy, who had run away to fight in the American Civil War. One thing only was he certain of in the future: he must go back to Africa alone.

7

ALONE IN AFRICA

"WILL Dr. Livingstone look for the sources of the Nile?" That challenge from the Royal Geographical Society was just what David wanted.

In Zanzibar he gathered his caravan. It was a wonderful collection of pack animals; camels, mules, donkeys and Indian water buffaloes. His two most trustful porters were his African friends Susi and Chuma.

They landed near to the mouth of the Rovuma in March 1866 and set off to tramp inland to Lake Nyasa. Through jungle bush, and the "steaming, smothering air" of the hot, dense, tropical forest, the caravan moved slowly. David was glad at last to get out on to the plateau, where the air was clear and the country open. On every side he saw signs of the slave trade. He saw women tied by the neck to trees, murdered when they could walk no further. In one village David freed a well dressed and stately looking woman who was held captive by an old man. The old man was about to sell her to the slave traders, but she shouted so loudly that David and his men stopped to listen to her story. She was on her way to her husband, she said, when the old man captured her. David gave the old man a cloth, and then took off the heavy slave stick round the woman's neck. She went with them and at every village she told the people what had happened to her. When they arrived at her own village she left them, but not before she told her husband and the whole village of what they had done for her.

High up the Rovuma valley, David was disappointed not to find a big inland waterway. Food was difficult to get, because of the slave traffic, and he and his men were often hungry. They reached Lake Nyasa on August 8, 1866. David wrote, "I felt grateful to the Hand that had protected us thus far on our journey. It was as if I had come back to an old home I had never expected to see again, and it was pleasant to bathe in the delicious waters once more, and hear the roar of the sea, and dash in the rollers. Temperature 71 deg. at 8 a.m., while the air was 65 deg. I felt quite exhilarated."

His plan was to cross the lake by native canoe or dhow, and then advance to the new country beyond, but he could get no one to ferry him over, for all the people were afraid of the slave traders. Therefore he had to march round the lake on to a high plateau above the water, where the air was clear and deliciously cool. As they went forward the rains came, the "set-in" rains as he called them, and made walking more difficult. Food was scarce and often he and his men were hungry. On Christmas Day, 1866, he lost his four goats, which meant that he was without milk to help him to digest his rough meal porridge. He was so hungry that at night he dreamed of dinners he had eaten and would like to eat. When David's stock of meal gave out he shared Simon's, his faithful servant, until he noticed that Simon too was going without food. Then, he says, "I tightened my belt by three holes to relieve the hunger."

They plodded on through the rain-sodden country, hungry and dispirited. Two of his men deserted him, taking his medicine chest with them. "I felt," he wrote, "as if I had received the sentence of death. All my other goods I had divided in case of loss, but never dreamed of losing the precious quinine and other remedies . . . It is difficult to say from the heart: Thy will be done. This loss of the medicine box gnaws at the heart terribly."

They stayed for some days at the village of Chief Chitapangwa. He sold them a cow and for the first time in six weeks they had enough to eat. The old chief was a rascal who bargained for everything.

"Look," he said, "I have pleased you and I have sold you a cow. Will you not please me and give me enough cloth to cover me?"

David replied, "I have given you enough to cover your biggest wife." They all laughed, but the chief kept on.

"Give me a blanket, and one of your boxes."

"I cannot do that for I have no boxes or blankets to spare."

"Your boys have blankets, give me one of them."

"No," replied David, "they are not slaves. The blankets belong to them."

"But you will make much money from your journey. You must pay me for passing through my land."

"I will not make money from this journey. I am going to find out where the great rivers rise. I am seeking a way to end the slave traffic. I come to tell your people about their Father, the great God."

"You may tell us about the Great God," the chief replied, "but," and he pulled down the under lid of his eye as if to say, "I don't believe you are not making money out of this."

At last they came to a ridge overlooking Lake Tanganyika. "I never saw anything so still and peaceful as it lies all the morning. In the north it seems to narrow into a gateway, but the people can tell us nothing about it. They suspect us. I am deeply thankful in having got so far."

He stayed at the lake for a fortnight thrilled by its beauty, and by the many animals on its shores. But David was very ill. Without medicine, and without quinine, his fever made him too weak to stand. He was glad to meet Mohammed bin Saleh, a tall, portly, black Arab with a pleasant smile and a pure white beard, who had traded for years in the area. He looked after David and gave him good food, and treated him with his own Arab medicine, and put him on the trail again. This time to find Lake Bangweulu.

David had very few goods left for barter and the Arabs strongly advised him not to make the journey. The country was under flood water, and for hours he waded through black, sticky mud. Yet he went on, hoping to find the source of the Nile. The country round about Lake Bangweulu was flat and treeless. Too ill to travel alone, and entirely dependent on his Arab friends, David trudged wearily on. The caravan was a strange mixture of people, the Arab and his friends, David and his five men, and strings of wretched slaves yoked together with heavy slave sticks. They carried ivory and copper, and some carried food. The rains were pitiless and David developed pneumonia. He coughed day and night, and finally could not walk. The Arabs carried him in a litter, and brought him back at last to Lake Tanganyika and Ujiji very tired and dreadfully thin.

Always restless he was soon off again towards the river Lualaba, some six hundred miles away. He had seen this river before and thought it might be part of the Nile. Teeming rain and lack of food, repeated attacks of malaria, and tribal slave trading wars, drove him back to Ujiji. As he was walking at the back of his party, in single file along a narrow jungle path, a huge spear came hurtling at him and grazed his back, then another whizzed past just in front of him. He came to a clearing in the forest, and saw a gigantic tree burning at its base, and just as he approached it began to topple over. He ran back and it crashed to the ground, just a yard behind him, covering him with twigs and dust.

At Ujiji all his goods had been stolen. He was down in health and in spirit. And then he says, "When my spirits were at their lowest ebb the Good Samaritan was close at hand, for one morning Susi came running at the top of his speed and gasped out, 'An Englishman. I see him,' and darted off to meet him. An American flag at the head of the caravan told the nationality of the stranger. Bales of goods, baths of tin, huge kettles, cooking pots, tents, etc., made me think 'This must be a luxurious traveller, and not one at his wits' end like me'."

It was Henry Morton Stanley, a reporter of the *New York Herald*, who had been sent out by his paper to find Dr. Livingstone, alive or dead, and if dead, then to bring back his body. He had found him, after a long trek, in October, 1871, and now as he approached David came forward to meet him.

They raised their hats, and Stanley says when he saw him, a pale, wearied man, with a grey beard, wearing a bluish cap with a faded gold band round it, and red sleeved waistcoat, he wanted to jump for joy; but instead he slowly said, "Dr. Livingstone, I presume."

"Yes," replied David.

"I thank God that I have been permitted to see you," said Stanley.

David answered with a twinkle in his eye, "I am very thankful I am here to welcome you."

Arabs and natives followed them and a great crowd of over a thousand people gathered outside David's hut. Eagerly David opened the bag of letters that Stanley had brought. Letters from his children lit his face with joy as he laid them aside to talk to his guest.

"You read your letters, don't mind me," said Stanley. But David quietly replied, "I have learnt patience. I have waited years for letters. I can surely wait a few hours longer. Tell me the news."

Stanley brought new life to David Livingstone. He shared his clothes and his medicine chest, and in order to get the sick man better he himself cooked food for him in the European style. As he had good food to eat, he got better, and within three weeks the two men were planning explorations together. They enjoyed one another's company for four months. Stanley admired David's gentleness, his patience, his sense of humour and his infectious laugh, and above all, his deep belief in the goodness of God and his confidence that all would come out right at last.

He tried to persuade David to go back with him, but he found him determined to finish alone his search for the Nile. So they parted— March 14, 1872—Stanley to tell the world that he had found David Livingstone; David, with a handful of African companions, to look again for the source of the Nile.

March 19 was his birthday. He wrote his birthday prayer: "My Jesus, my king, my life, my all. Once more I dedicate my whole self to Thee. Accept me and grant, O gracious Father, that ere this year is gone, I may finish my task. In Jesus' name I ask it. Amen, so let it be. David Livingstone."

He was sure that he was just about to discover

where the great river rose. In fact, on a map
he had sent back with Stanley he had marked
"four fountains" south of Lake Bangweulu,
two of which flow northwards to Egypt, and
the other two south. He made up his mind
to get once more to the lake, and find
them. With sixty men and plenty of stores
sent up by Stanley he was ready to tackle the
oozing, boggy "sponges", around Lake Bangweulu.

By November he was back on his old trail
to Lake Bangweulu, from the north. Unceasing
rain, squelching bogs and heavy clouds which
made it impossible to take readings from the
sun or the moon, held him up.

"I don't know where we are," he wrote, "and
the people are deceitful." Week after week he
plodded on through the sweltering marshes.
He suffered from dysentery, and loss of blood,
and could feel himself getting weaker. Then
he discovered that something was wrong with
the silvering of his sextant, and his readings
were not accurate. His local guides were of no
use, and the chiefs were unreliable.

Matipa, an old chief, promised him canoes to take his party over the vast flooded plains which stretched before them as far as the eye could see. The canoes never came. At last David took action. With his men he walked into Matipa's village, and strode into his house. He fired his pistol through the roof of the house, and called his men to come. Matipa fled to another village. David then ordered three canoes which were brought at once. His party embarked, and "punted for six hours and landed in pitiless pelting rain. The loads were all soaked, and with the cold it was bitterly uncomfortable."

He was so weak now that he could not walk, and his men carried him. Yet he made his observations. He noted that the rainfall of seventy-three inches was higher than any he had found elsewhere; the amount of water amazed him, and he wondered if the Nile, which was famous for flooding in Egypt, did the same thing at its source.

Still losing blood, he had to be carried. The rain was so heavy that one night his tent was torn into shreds, and he remarked with dry humour, "It is not all pleasure, this exploration."

He kept on and he recorded what he saw. "The river Lokulu," he writes, "is about thirty yards broad, very deep and flowing in marshes, two knots from the south-south-east to north-north-west, into the lake." But this was his last detailed entry. It is dated April 20.

The next few scribbled notes tell of his increasing weakness. On the evening of 27 April his men built a little hut for him, and made a bed of sticks and grass. He lay on it unable to move. Three days later the Chief Chitambo called to see him, but he could speak only a few words, and asked him to call back the next day.

That night David called the faithful Susi and asked, "How far is it to Lualaba?"

"It is three days away," Susi said.

He groaned, "Oh dear, oh dear," and dozed. He called Susi again to bring his medicine chest, and struggled to take a dose of calomel.

Then in a weak voice he said, "All right, you can go now."

The boy, watching at the door of his hut, saw his master on his knees by his bed, saying his prayers. He was holding his last conversation, for when they came in the early morning they found him still on his knees, with his body stretched forward, and his head held in his hands. He had gone on to speak with his Master face to face. It was May 1, 1873.

His men gathered together to decide what they should do. They dried his thin wasted body in the sun, and then embalmed it. They took out his heart and buried it in one of the tin boxes under a mulva tree. Jacob Wainwright, who had joined him with the carriers Stanley had sent from the coast, could speak a little English, and he read the burial service from the Book of Common Prayer, and they fired their guns in salute over his grave. Wainwright carved David Livingstone's name in deep letters on the tree and Chief Chitambo promised to guard it.

Then gently wrapping his body, with his legs bent up, they packed it so that it looked like a bale of calico. Sewn up in sailcloth and slung on a pole, the burden was reverently hoisted to the carriers' shoulders.

Susi and Chuma, the most experienced of the boys, led the way back to the coast, determined that David should be buried with his own people. This famous march by African men showed how much they honoured and loved their leader. At Lake Tanganyika they were met by a British expeditionary force, searching for Livingstone, and when the leader heard the news he ordered the body to be buried, but the Africans would not allow it. Chuma cried out, "No, no, very big man, cannot bury here."

At last they reached a British Consul who arranged to ship the body to England. They had carried it 1500 miles, and it had taken them nine months. They sailed with their precious burden, and arrived in Southampton on April 15, 1874. It lay in state, and on Saturday, April 18, David Livingstone was buried in Westminster Abbey. It was a day of national mourning. His friends were there—Dr. Kirk, Dr. Moffat, Mr. Oswell and others, and Jacob Wainwright was also there, with Susi and Chuma. They brought him to his resting place.

David Livingstone never discovered the source of the Nile, but before his body had reached the coast Dr. Kirk had persuaded the Sultan of Zanzibar to sign a treaty which closed the slave market in Zanzibar and banned the sea route. Within a few years the slave trade had ended, and Africa was open to Christianity and Commerce.